From the desktop of Jeffrey Simmons

A vacation in Paris inspired Miroslav Sasek to create childrens travel guides to the big cities of the world. He brought me *This is Paris* in 1958 when I was publishing in London, and we soon followed up with *This is London*. Both books were enormously successful, and his simple vision grew to include more than a dozen books. Their amusing verse, coupled with bright and charming illustrations, made for a series unlike any other, and garnered Sasek (as we always called him) the international and popular acclaim he deserved.

I was thrilled to learn that *This is Venice* will once again find its rightful place on bookshelves. Sasek is no longer with us (and I have lost all contact with his family), but I am sure he would be delighted to know that a whole new generation of wide-eyed readers is being introduced to his whimsical, imaginative and enchanting world.

Your name here

Published by arrangement with Simon & Schuster Books for Young Readers,
Simon & Schuster Children's Publishing Division

This edition first published in 2005 by
UNIVERSE PUBLISHING
A Division of Rizzoli International Publications, Inc.
300 Park Avenue South
New York, NY 10010
www.rizzoliusa.com

*See updated Venice facts at end of book

2010 / 10 9 8 7 6 5

Printed in China

ISBN: 978-0-7893-1223-5

Library of Congress Catalog Control Number: 2004110229

Cover design: centerpointdesign
Universe editor: Jane Newman

M·SASEK

This is
VENICE

UNIVERSE

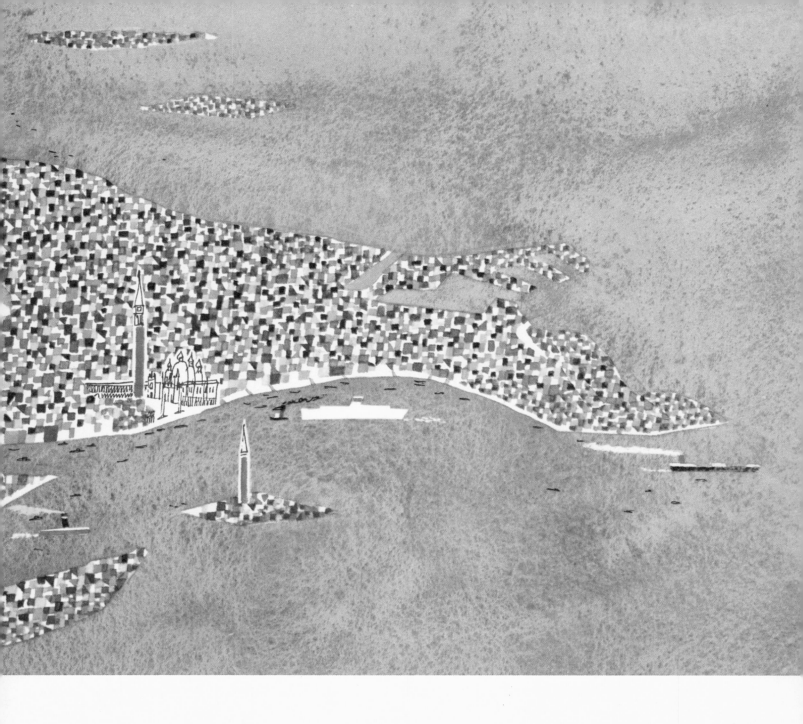

Venice, built between the sixth and eighth centuries by fugitives from mainland barbarians on an invisible forest of inverted tree trunks, lies in its lovely lagoon like a great dolphin. It became a powerful republic, the home of famous mariners, merchants, statesmen and artists.

A Venetian motto could well be, "Abandon wheels, all ye who enter here."

After crossing the two-and-a-quarter mile causeway from the mainland —

travelers by train abandon their wheels at the station:

travelers by car or bus at the Piazzale Roma.

That's why the Piazza San Marco will never look like this.

Venice is wedded to the water, to the Adriatic, which has given her freedom and wealth.

This is "Bucintoro" on which the Venetians used to re-enact each year the marriage between the city and the sea.

They built Venice on 117 little islands reinforced by millions of pilings. Four hundred bridges span the 177 canals.

In their streets —

this is the only traffic.

All else

is waterbound:

the petrol station —

street cleaners —

taxis —

buses —

vaporetto:

motoscafo:

motonave.

The water brings scenery to the theatre —

melons to the housewives —

and tourists to Venice.

On the water things begin —

and end —

subject to the Highway Code.

As much as Venice loves the water, the water loves Venice

— and periodically proves it.

The Venetians are ready for these shows of affection.

But there are times when the sea gets out of hand.

The water is also Venice's enemy. It weakens the foundations of the campanili —

yet most of the palaces, fragile and lacelike, manage to stand undisturbed.

Palazzo Contarini del Bovolo.

Venetian specialties —

glass:

lace:

seafood:

and house-numbering.

In each of the six districts of Venice every
door has a number, even those which are
no longer doors.

"Gondola! . . . Gondola! . . . Gondola! . . . Gondola! . . . Gondola! . . . Gondola! . . .

The most romantic way to see the city.

Length: 36 feet; width: 5 feet; weight: 1350 pounds; cost: that of a car.

ndola! . . . Gondola! . . . Gondola! . . . Gondola!"

In the sixteenth century there were ten thousand
gondolas in Venice, today a mere five hundred.*

Eight different kinds of wood are used to build a gondola.

The most romantic time to see Venice is in the evening.

"Ganzers" are armed with boat hooks. They pull the gondolas to the shore and assist passengers to alight.

The most romantic sight is the Grand Canal at night.

The Canal Grande, two-and-a-half miles long, the main street of Venice, is bordered by more than a hundred marble palaces of many styles and ages.

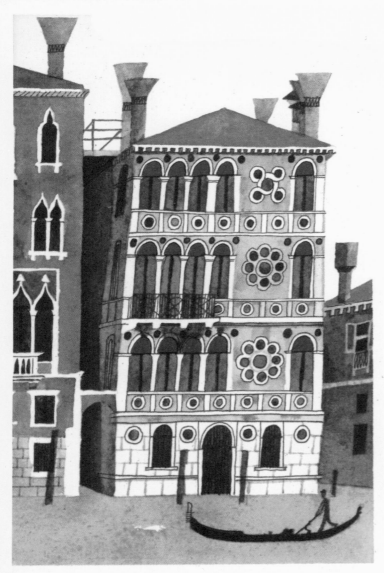

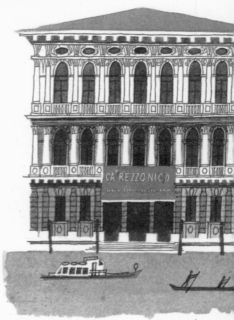

Ca'Rezzonico, built by Longhena in the seventeenth century, housing the city's collection of eighteenth-century works of art.

Palazzo Dario — fifteenth century — called "The Old Lady of the Jewels."

Palazzo Vendramin-Calergi — fifteenth century — where Richard Wagner spe his last days and died in 1883.

Palazzo Grassi — eighteenth century — is now an International Centre for Arts and Costume.

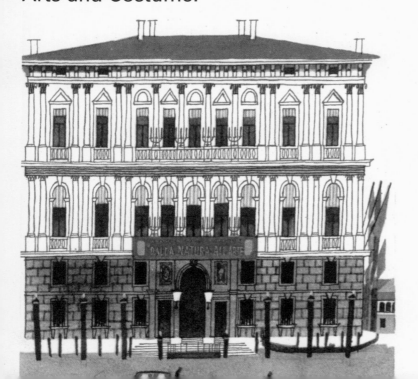

Ca'Foscari — fifteenth century — the seat of the University Institute of Economics and Commerce.

Ca'd'Oro, "The Golden House" — fifteenth century — the most beautiful palace of them all.

This is the best known of the Grand Canal's three bridges —
the Rialto.

Near one end of the bridge you will find the "Erberia" market and the little church of San Giacomo, traditionally the oldest one in Venice.

Near the other end, in Campo San Bartolomeo, the statue of the Venetians' beloved playwright, Carlo Goldoni. The pigeons like him too.

But the best-liked meeting place for the local pigeons is —

Piazza San Marco,

one of the most beautiful squares in the world.

      The Basilica of St. Mark, built in the Byzantine style, adorned by

      43,000 square feet of mosaics, mainly in gold.

The campanile is 323 feet high.

In 1902 the original tower collapsed.

No entry to the basilica for tourists improperly dressed.

When the "Moors" on the Clock Tower strike 9 A.M. or 2 P.M. —

the pigeons of Venice are
fed by an official —

but at other times by the tourists.*

A feed for the pigeons means a photo for
the album, so the pigeons artfully pose.

Your pigeon picture is one of the famous souvenirs.

These chaps will supply you with others.

You will find them around the Doges' Palace —

and around the Loggetta, in other times the
meeting place of the patricians.

For eleven hundred years the Doges' Palace housed the
Government of the Venetian Republic.
Here 120 Doges succeeded one another in office between
697 and 1797.

The winged lion atop the marble column
is the symbol of St. Mark, which has become
the symbol of Venice.

In the Doges' Palace, on the wall of the Great
Council Chamber, Tintoretto painted his "Paradise."
It is the largest painting in the world: 72 feet by 22 feet.

In 1594 Tintoretto died in this house,
No. 3399, Fondamenta dei Mori.

Across the Bridge of Sighs
prisoners used to be led from
the jail to the Doges' Palace.

When you have taken a picture
of the bridge, you can turn
around and snap —

San Giorgio Maggiore, a sixteenth-century masterpiece by
Palladio, on an island of its own.

Santa Maria della Salute, built by Longhena in the seventeenth century.
1,200,000 hardwood pilings were needed to reinforce its foundations.

This is the Accademia di Belle Arti, which contains by far the most important collection of Venetian paintings.

But in Venice you can find famous paintings also in all the churches.

The Church of the Frari, built around 1250,
contains Titian's celebrated painting of the
"Assumption."

The Church of Santi Giovanni e Paolo, the "Pantheon of the Doges," disputes with the Frari the foremost place among the Gothic brick churches of Venice.

When sight-seeing in Venice in hot summer,
this is one way to quench your thirst.*

This is how the horses at the Lido
keep off the sun.*

The tourists imitate the horses —

but the Venetians don't.

At the end of your stay don't forget to pick up
THE photograph for your family album!

THIS IS VENICE...TODAY!

*Page 31: Today there are fewer than 500 gondolas in Venice.

*Page 47: Today the pigeons in Piazza San Marco are no longer fed by an official, but you can buy corn at kiosks and feed them yourself!

*Page 58: Today you will no longer see watermelon stands in Venice. However, many vendors sell fruit salad to keep you cool in the summer. And there haven't been horses at the Lido since the 1980s.